Eternity Lost
and Other Poems

ROY K. PIPER

Printed in the United States of America

First Printing, 2015

ISBN 978-0-9903300-3-5

CONTENTS

Eternity Lost and Other Poems

Roy K. Piper is a fearless poet. Unafraid to use traditional rhyme and meter in this modern era, *ETERNITY LOST and Other Poems* gives us thoughtful stories and meditations of whales and squirrels, Shakespeare and Frost, and even Jessica Fletcher of Murder, She Wrote. Even Godzilla! In the title poem, he challenges us to confront "the terrible toll" of environment. Read the man's work, and you will appreciate the ordinary and the extraordinary aspects of your life.

—John T. Hitchner, author of the collections *Seasons and Shadows, Pieces of Life Between,* and the novel *The Acolyte*.

Roy K. Piper has been documenting his piece of America for decades writing lines like these:

"Next, the blast from the Amtrak makes my van sway and shake as a skiff rocks at the dockside from a powerboat's wake."

Enjoy.

—Norman Klein, a founding editor of *Ploughshares*

ETERNITY LOST
A fantasy poem about the environment

Part I   INTRODUCTION   April 1989

So—I once had a vision, a dream, or a spell,
in which I did not really feel very well;
I relinquished my hold on all tangible worth
and departed this ancient and animate earth.

But since skeptical all of my life had been I
of afterlife being should one ever die,
unexpected it was to be fully aware
of rational consciousness happening there.

And still being somewhat adventurous bent,
astonished was I to have found myself sent
by some most fantastic finagle of fate,
to be standing in awe at a nacreous gate.

A geezer appeared, shook my hand, and he said,
"There's nothing up here that you're going to dread,
providing your psyche's brave attitude minds
whatever the judgment a lay jury finds."

This thought quite allayed all my whimsical fears,
for I've nothing to fear from a jury by peers.
But peers? It appears that the pool only features
extinct or endangered-most wilderness creatures.

ETERNITY LOST
A fantasy poem about the environment

Part II   THE PANEL

They read me my rights such as those of Miranda,
delivered in course by a pompous old panda;
then feeling quite helpless I stood like a fool
as the powers of Heaven presented the pool:

There were whooping cranes, dodos, rhinoceros too,
passenger pigeons, and a whale called Blue.
a mountain gorilla, a grizzly brown bear,
then a tiger, a cheetah, and a puma were there.

An American bison, a giant eland,
along with a leopard, were also on hand.
A couple of condors aroost in a tree
were casting malevolent glances at me.

I pondered what ethical trial I might merit
as prairie dogs chummed with a black footed ferret,
and a battered old bighorn with coat gray and worn
was scratching a young cougar's back with its horn.

An African elephant mournfully sang
as it waltzed all around with a wolf and orang.
From out of this group there were chosen some twelve,
that into my natural history would delve.

Re: Prince Charles' endangered species list

ETERNITY LOST
A fantasy poem about the environment

Part III   INTERLUDE

"Hold on," complained I, "This can hardly be fair;
with this kind of jury I haven't a prayer."
Said the geezer, "O please, Sir, you'll have to believe
we are doing our best to be honest, so we've
assigned an attorney, a lawyer you'll like."
And, lo, there appeared my old setter dog, Mike.

"Why Mike," uttered I as I blinked back a tear,
"So what in high heaven are you doing here?
No angel were you in your lush earthly life.
You chased after cats and caused general strife
molesting the skunks, dumping garbage from cans,
and barking with vigor at autos and vans."

"Look," he said calmly, "you're missing the point;
it is not petty crime in this uppity joint
that ever has taken the terrible toll
of any deserving one's ultimate soul.
I've been much around and I've learned all the ropes,
and probably, therefore, can bolster your hopes.
As for life down on earth, this is not quite the same;
what matters the most is how you played the *game*."

ETERNITY LOST
A fantasy poem about the environment

Part IV   THE TRIAL

I could tell by his tone that there was no escape;
and then there was my life as on video tape,
where the highlights were shown in the frankest detail
in such color that made even sunsets look pale,
since they wanted to know in "ahead" and "reverse"
whether I'd made the world end up better or worse.

Had I killed for necessity, only to eat
or defend my own life if I couldn't retreat?
Had I ever for profit's expedient haste
desecrated the earth with a poisonous waste?
Had I in a benevolent manner behaved
so that maybe an animal's life had been saved...?

Then they saw on a sidewalk right after a rain
that I plucked a poor earthworm from where it had lain,
and tossed it to lawn where its life had begun
before it could dry to a crisp in the sun.

They nodded and said, "Who could act in this fashion
surely possesses a mote of compassion;
but we're stymied by having an evidence lack,
so, as for this person we're sending him back."

ETERNITY LOST
A fantasy poem about the environment

Part V   FINALE—AFTERTHOUGHTS

I thanked good old Mike for my timely reprieve;
his film clip, though valid, was hard to perceive.
At best, anyhow, I got out on probation
with hopes to enlighten the rest of the nation.

Is human life sacred? Does anyone know?
We invented the gods that are telling us so.
Would an unbiased deity way off in space
ever give human beings a favorite place
when it sees us destroying the land and the seas
and killing the fauna whenever we please?

Despite some good people aware of this curse
who are actively seeking the trend to reverse,
colossal conceit seems to hound humankind
to reason acuity chanced in the mind
should give us the right to use all of our powers
to claim that the world is exclusively ours.

Must we occupy habitat, every square foot,
with ourselves, our constructions, our garbage and soot,
and always be crowding our way to the top?
Like the fabled old salt mill, we—can't—make—us—stop!

THE WINDOW TO MY MIND
October 31, 1992

It is no one else's business what I think;
My personal philosophies are held
Inviolable and not to be dispelled.
Be I, though, relaxed a bit by drink,
A clever one might read my blush or blink,
But never shall I quickly be propelled
Divulging what I am cautiously compelled
To guard as with an armor's iron link.

Yet, sometimes comes a chink in this reserve,
When inner thoughts may seek their way in verse,
And sneakily come spewing out, I find;
For poetry, eroder of my nerve,
Robber of resolve, or even worse,
Becomes an open window to my mind.

FORSYTHIA   1988

Forsythia, your brilliant yellow bloom
well brash glorifies a sunny April day.
Your, mid-spectrum, radiant display
then helps dispel the winter's dark and gloom.
For when the tepid rains and thunder's boom
remove the ice and snow for skate and sleigh
and spring's awaited show is underway,
your cheerful hue ensures the winter's doom.
Yet, once we felt December warm as May
when Indian summer lingered overlong
you showed your color, brazen, bright, and bold,
though not achieving spring's unique array
and autumn for your flower seemed somehow wrong,
you did defy the pending season's cold.

THE WHALES   November, 1988

At a bay far northernmost on Alaska's arctic coast
paused some whales while in their annual migration;
but their leisure pace together with some early frigid weather
has caused the world a massive consternation.

As the episode unveils, we see California whales
trapped by ice within the freezing bay;
without a space to blow, soon everyone should know,
they'll perish sure as morning brings the day.

But what is really counting is the rescue that is mounting
and the effort against the climate that is hurled;
for people never pause to pursue a worthy cause
involving soon the nations of the world.

To effect this hopeful cause there are men with poles and saws
out cutting holes for access to the air.
When this futile effort fails, upon the scene there sails
a mighty ship to clear the passage bare.

One tends to wonder why they would ever make a try
at attempting this commendable endeavor
in a place so far remote that it rarely sees a boat
excepting in the best of summer weather.

MORELS DEBUNKED   May 1990

I have a certain love I'm loath to share,
a love for certain fungi, very rare,
that only for a day or two in May
emerge from the earth in order to convey
their spores by wind to wooded hill or dell.
I allude to the delectable morel.

A man who knows a place these mushrooms grow,
and harbors anxious fear lest others know,
will guard his secret jealously as life
from everyone, including his dear wife;
for the only real secret that is true,
is what is known by one and not by two.

But, when it comes to basic honesty
and fine morels be judged for quality,
they're very good, as wild mushrooms go,
perhaps the best of all I have had, although,
the mushrooms I enjoy as much, or more,
are mushrooms bought in any grocery store.

GRAY SQUIRREL   1991

Little friend, whom I delight to see,
I have long admired your fluid, agile, grace,
your fearless leaps to travel tree to tree,
your cutesy look and of course, your tireless pace.

Our old cat, which terrorized the lot
of chipmunks, and ingested quite a few,
with ever due respect it never fought
nor hardly dared to square off with you.

Some people think your most relentless chore
is caching acorns all around the yard
by digging little holes in which to store
the nuts until the quest for food comes hard.

No way I say, the acorn in your face
shows deliberate and solitary aim
of planting oak trees all around the place—
a process which to me becomes a game:

For with ensuing summer as they sprout
in garden, lawn, or shrubs, to my chagrin,
then I must mow or try to weed them out—
but elsewhere you are ever sure to win.

And win you should, the oak that lifts my fence
is actually a long-term dinner tray
to feed your many generations hence.
Every day to squirrels is Arbor Day.

Published in *THE POETS' TOUCHSTONE*

AUGUST EXONERATED
(Erma, go blah!)

March 31, 1991

A columnist of much renown once wrote
that August is the dullest time of year,
its dismal weeks of purposes unclear
reduce the blahs to even lower note
without a holiday as antidote;
a useless month so fraught with heat to sear
the very earth as its crematory bier—
redeeming factors seemingly remote.
Not so, say I, with statement resolute,
for August is the culmination of
those many months of wearisome endeavor,
the time when local gardens furnish fruit,
the savory abundance that we love.
Let August be epitomized forever!

Published in THE POETS' TOUCHSTONE

LITTLE SKUNK   August 28, 1992

Little skunk, your digging in my lawn
In quest of beetle grubs, your nightly feed,
Suggests of one possessing much more brawn,
Or maybe there's an army of your breed.

For each and every morning I'm appalled
To see the excavations that you dig;
You must be using some machine that's called
A payloader, or some such digging rig.

All right, I had to years ago decide,
And chose to go the natural process route:
Refraining from a harsh insecticide
A decision I'll consider to refute.

But somehow, conscience does not yet allow
A war on other innocent bugs and worms;
Perhaps you've eaten all the grubs by now,
And you and I can come to peaceful terms.

If you were sent by some revengeful god
To plague an unrepentant golfer who
Neglects replacing divots to the sod,
Well listen up, and hear my plea to you.

Why me, an honest, innocent, worthy type,
Who labors hard from summer into fall
To guide his lawn and garden to get ripe
For looks and food but plays no golf at all?

THE CUTWORM'S VIEWPOINT   August 6, 1993
(regarding farmers)

In May you spade the resting earth,
  its long siesta ended;
you work the soil for all you're worth,
  with nutrients expended.

You plant your seeds in hills and rows,
  and in the space allotted
you place, where last year's vegetables froze,
  new plants already potted.

Then when the new seeds germinate
  so likewise do the weeds;
and that's when I anticipate
  to satisfy my needs.

You tend your garden all day long
  with conscientious care,
as if it were a sinful wrong:
  a weed left anywhere.

Though mulch is fine in outspread heaps,
  there is a better choice:
a weedy cover also keeps
  the garden soil moist.

But no, you have to till until
  there's nothing else for me;
and I am forced to eat my fill
  of vegetables, you see.

For this you want to take my life
  without the hint of a trial,
and slice me up with a pruning knife
  to enrich the compost pile.

BUGS   October 1997

Some insects, it seems, just do not aim to please;
they delight in inflicting some fatal disease.
But why do we make such a furious fuss
when insects attempt to exterminate us?
All they are doing is paying us back
for tons of insecticide spread by the sack;
or even a whack that's delivered by hand
could cause a bug union to make a demand
that we are unfair in the way that we treat them
when we kill them for spite and do not even eat them.
And so they all along ought to plead self-protection
as can we, in our turn, with a smug introspection:
As in all forms of life there are good guys and bad guys;
a stinging thing may just be bad in disguise.
But mostly with bugs we are downright annoyed
and feel that such creatures should all be destroyed.
We are bigger than they are but badly outnumbered,
while natural defense leaves us sadly encumbered.
Hard work in the lab keeps us holding our own
in a no-win condition, the future unknown.

LIMERICK   August, 1990

Once a young Sag Harbor tailor,
when offered a berth on a whaler,
said, "I don't want to go
if I can't sew, and so,
I'm really not much of a sailor."

THE OLD TREE ROW   October 30, 1994

Those ancient maple trees that stand in row,
though most mature, if even still alive
with gnarled and broken boles that ceased to grow,
are relics of a former farmstead drive.
The rotted trunks reveal sometimes when pried
the tap holes where once wooden sap pails hung;
and bits of wire protruding from the side
betray the course a pasture fence was strung.
The mowing and the pasture now are grown
with forests reaching to the maples' height;
the drive is but a path the chipmunks own;
the trees but homes for bugs' and birds' delight.
A fertile place for some biologist,
but I regret the role of eulogist.

Published in *THE POETS' TOUCHSTONE*

BARKING DOG   September 9, 1991

Barking dog, your efforts audible
wrench my every nerve from scalp to toe.
Your baritone to you sounds laudable;
to me it's but a grating cause of woe.
You scare my child, and now my cat's gone wild;
the chickens in the yard have run amok.

In spite of this, I may be reconciled—
resisting thoughts involving yonder rock—
and contemplate this weighty matter through:
You're saying with your raucous barking spell
that, in these times, it's your only job to do!
And must I say, you really do it well.

INDIFFERENCE   July 31, 1996

The extraordinary beauty of a rose
has long been praised by poets and their ilk;
all of which seems normal, I suppose,
but beauty may invoke a trend to bilk.
We seem to overlook the vicious thorn,
which unremorsefully lacerates my hide,
till literally and figuratively torn,
I cannot opt to favor either side.
So once when summer rains exceeded need,
and fungus-blighted leaves dropped off the stems,
a few remaining buds, though, tried indeed
to strive as trellis-decorating gems.
They could be saved by fungicidal dust,
but nowhere is it written that I must.

WINTER SOLITUDE   May, 1998

While pausing in the woods one day I found
in nature, for a pleasant interlude,
the closest thing to perfect solitude.
It was January, calm, without a sound;
no other living creatures were around,
as if they felt it rude should they intrude
in any way upon the tranquil mood,
nor even make a track on the snowy ground.
The spell persisted half an hour or more,
the stillness that of some unopened cave,
until at last I thought I could discern
amongst the topmost limbs, on daily tour
a tiny chickadee, its spirit brave,
awakening the woods to life's return.

Published in *THE POETS' TOUCHSTONE*

GODZILLA   1999

On chaises at the pool we lazed supine
and peacefully watched a gecko from the weeds
venture across the deck in hopes to dine
on flies, or any fare on which it feeds.

Now, everything is relative in scale;
a tiny lizard likens to a fly
as baleen whales stack up against the krill,
or vicious barracuda to the fry.

Since this was our excitement for the day,
nature thus provided us a thriller;
and in this connotation, anyway,
we gave the little guy the name "Godzilla"

But when we came to greet our friend next day,
while hoping he'd emerge soon from the shrubs,
an egret, to our horrified dismay,
wandered closely through the trees and stubs.

The gecko on a palm trunk quickly scampered
around the tree to flee the hungry lance,
which reached around on a neck so far unhampered
that poor Godzilla didn't stand a chance.

Well, why should human beings be immune
from predators which also need to eat?
A crocodile in every pool and soon
our overpopulation might deplete.

DISILLUSIONED   August 31, 1992

Enthralled, I watch her pass along the street,
her radiant beauty emanating grace,
a cheerful smile adorns the pretty face;
her tasteful garments, vivid but discreet,
enhance her perfect figure, head to feet.
Her glistening hair shines bright without a trace
of artificialness that could displace
my pleasant, heartfelt, warming, cost-free treat.

Oh no! No don't! Don't light that cigarette!
Do not step off your pedestal so soon.
I cannot stop you, drat it, if you must
so utterly destroy my sweet vignette
and quickly change from angel to buffoon.
Shattered joys are woefully unjust.

THE SMILE April 4, 1994

A little child who makes an ugly face
may be told that she could freeze that way,
grotesquely, in a permanent display,
and spend her life in abject ill disgrace.
So, could we make a correlative case
of one whose smile spreads cheer like a sunshine's ray
and then endures, as firmly fired in clay
to spread its warmth to every dismal place?
I know not who she was nor what her cause,
just saw her bear her grin for several hours,
staunchly persevering in her pride
by blandly clenching unrelenting jaws
to broadcast all her charismatic powers—
But I wondered: was she happy deep inside?

RAWTHER May 6, 1995, cauda May 30, 2012

He much admired her cultivated speech;
her accent, toned in everything she said,
indicated one most highly bred,
a blue-blood through and through, a peerless peach.
Though her reserve was difficult to breach,
he plotted crafty strategy which led
to closest friendship—possibly to wed—
a lofty goal and feasible to reach.
So, one fine day at cocktail hour they sat,
she with white kid gloves, a stylish hat
and Dior dress for everyone to see.
They sipped their whiskey sours, one, two, three;
but with the alcohol in blood increase,
her accent slowly changed to... Javanese.

      Not Brooklynese—
Use any means to meet the poet's plight:
attempting to avoid one's being trite.

AS WHEN BUTTERFLIES EMERGE
October 26, 2002

A memory from the time of middle school:
A favorite so-called evidence of spring
was not the fragrant flowers blossoming;
azaleas, tulips, iris, as a rule,
were harbingers themselves in miniscule.
Ah no, a young man felt a pleasant zing
as girls in gorgeous garb became the thing;
when warm and sunny days became the tool
to free them from their winter-drab cocoons.
And boys perceived a glimmering of thought
that maybe some far day without duress
these lovely creatures in such flowery dress
are people too, whose friendships might be sought
for joining them in distant honeymoons.

RACE TRACK   1989

We went to the race track one night when we found
nothing better to do than watch horses run 'round.
And feeling the spirit the horsy crowd sets,
we provided ourselves with some money for bets:
A ten spot in pocket for fun at the track,
playing five of the races at two bucks a crack.
The plan was to wager the favorites to show,
and with anything left at the end have a go
at betting a long shot to win on the nose,
expecting to lose it, of course, at the close.
Any wins at the start would be welcome events,
though a two dollar bet might collect fifteen cents.
But after five races 'twas not very funny;
not a one "favorite" horse even ran in the money;
though we didn't hope for much and we didn't play it shrewdly,
then why did we have to be treated so rudely?
A fool and his money are parted quite slickly;
he sadly resents that they do it so quickly.
Some twenty five years ago thus we got burned,
and somehow or other we've never returned.

ON GIRL-WATCHING   August 9, 1991

Excuse me please, it's rude of me to stare!
Far be it from a crude attempt to flirt,
but should you feel my gazing be overt,
then I deserve your castigating swear.
The reason is that nearly everywhere,
with beauty such as yours I can't avert
my eyes from such a sumptuous dessert,
addicted, as it were, to one so fair.
Well, vivid sunsets, gorgeous flowers, and all
the masterworks of art throughout the years
do not resent their beauty be on view.
Yet, I must finally force my eyes to fall
and thus abide by rules in proper spheres,
but hope, deep down, you are not resentful too.

LATE AFTERNOON   1991

Late afternoon in summer comes a spell
when land surveyors find it good to work;
as coolness comes with mercy to repel
the midday's shimmering heat annoying quirk
of targets dancing in the reticle hairs.
The chief, perhaps, becomes a nervous wreck;
with atmospheric turmoil he despairs
of any accurate angulation check.
But, as the calmness settles in at length,
he may remain until the close of day
to take advantage of the waxing strength
of angles measured clearly by delay.

So similarly I look in broader scope
at life as it sneaks past middle age,
and see with certain clarity and hope
achievements and events I wish to gauge:
accomplishments that may reflect with pride—
or, scrutinized with unobstructed eye,
there may be some I'd much prefer to hide.
For in youth's early bustle I defy
all persons with decisions to be certain
they have made the wisest choices that they could;
and when the darkness drops the final curtain,
at least by then I shall know just where I stood.

Published in the Poetry Society of New Hampshire's
anthology *You Must Remember This*

ON SHAVING   November 16, 1993

Grandpa could, before the shaving stand,
hold a straightedged razor to his face
and shave with ease by using either hand
with equal skill of ambidextrous grace.
My father had it somewhat easier, though;
the safety razor, as a point to sell,
eliminated any need to know
the skill of honing edges very well.
My generation has it easier still:
electric razors came into the fore.
The process has progressed so far until
shaving is no burden, pain nor chore.
So why, with such efficiency on call,
young men today choose not to shave at all?

ODORS   September 30, 1993

The acuteness that defines the canine nose
is evolutionary opulence,
which in a dog may far exceed the sense
of eyesight to distinguish food or foes.
But, to a dog, as odor comes and goes,
is any essence apt to give offense—?
Or be enjoyed as peoples' frankincense?
Is something decomposed just a canine's rose?
Since dissonance does not destroy the ears
nor ugliness cause damage to the eyes,
then smell was analyzed as best I could
when a three-year-old, in innocence of years—
and causing thus this trend to rationalize—
said, "Granddad, you do not smell very good".

STATUE OF LIBERTY December 17, 1989

A statue stands out in the bay
with incredible things it can say,
like, people in strife
can find a new life,
and hope that they make it okay.

A WEEK BEFORE CHRISTMAS   1994
(A grandfather's side of a dialog with his married children)

Now look, you kids, don't try to do for me
what we had done for many a Christmas past.
It's really just a waste of time, you see,
to try to make those early customs last.
When you were small, well, that was different then;
Christmas is for children to have fun
and not for fogies acting young again.
We've done our job, and now our duty's done.

For when we're older we get feeling that
inertia is so hard to overcome
the season of Noel becomes old hat,
habitual, trite, a bore, and bothersome.
So spend your time with your own families now;
go shop and wrap and cook and decorate
where efforts such as you make, I'll allow,
won't be a total waste, at any rate.

How's that? You're going to trim that little tree?
You're not put off by this old cynic's spiel?
You'll go ahead with this in spite of me,
and Christmas time with me has some appeal?
OK, then, if you think I might be missed
and there's a comfy chair in which to plop,
I'll join you on that day , if you insist.
By golly, I shall even go and shop.

THE ENTROPY TWINS   1994

A simple definition I have read,
that entropy may be defined as this:
Transition from an ordered state, it said,
to one where all goes totally amiss;
all universal matter will resolve
along a one-way process, it explains,
degenerating, trying to evolve,
until, and finally, only chaos reigns.

Now, two young guys, some grandchildren of mine,
are agents to effect the said transition,
for entropy to them is sheer design—
while needing urgent will for ammunition.
A box of blocks reclining on a shelf
must promptly be inverted on the floor;
a deck of cards must never in itself
be left unstrewn amid torn teddy's gore.

A thousand Jackstones lurk about the rug,
like a fakir's most unyielding bed of nails;
a slimy plastic snake, a worm, or bug
adds everything but the smell of garbage pails.
As a purpose to their lives, or holy quest,
they create the most disorder ever seen.
Aware that they achieve their dismal best,
despair!—they've got my own chaotic gene.

A GIFT TO WALTER January 6, 1984

Old McWalter bought a farm,
and we all thought it could do no harm
to give a cat, a cow, or mutt,
a pig, a mule or something, but
instead of stock that's large and hairy,
why not give a gorgeous aviary?
 Because, after all, that rooster vane,
resplendent on its roof domain,
could point the wind for years and years,
yet harbor silent inner fears
of loneliness; for there he hovers
and pines away for need of lovers.
So, fear ye not, thou mighty bird,
your phobic cravings now are heard;
and with each morning's golden dawn,
way down below on Walter's lawn
(and we don't care if he can't bear 'em)*
you'll view your loving, strutting harem.

*Plastic lawn ornaments such as flamingos and ducks.

TO SHAKESPEARE

February 30, 1990

It is with deep respect and high regard,
and in a humble mood of praise that I
commemorate the well renowned Bard
with reverence and perhaps a wistful sigh.
For who but He, in words of beauty rare
could pen His piece with eloquence and then
in different words of equal skill and care
repeat His theme as notably again,
while mortal poets, in their quest to write,
confront the stubborn versifying wall,
though coping with the challenge of their plight
are struggling to express themselves at all?
Then how dare I, mere poet of the norm,
how dare I try to emulate His form!?

Published in *THE POETS' TOUCHSTONE*

ELABORATION ON THE THEME OF

HOME SWEET HOME   1988

To a person born on a prairie farm
   who ventures forth from home,
A forest crest may produce distress
   by obscuring the starry dome,
And rising seas from a blustery breeze
   cause gastronomic ills,
Or he could feel caged and perhaps enraged
   by some claustrophobic hills.

To the mountain man, on the other hand,
    who opts to see the world,
The prairie space is a dreary place,
    just to watch as the windmills whirled.
I have traveled some as a roaming bum,
    as a soldier, and a tourist,
With discontent where the suitcase went
    and no claim to be a purist.

Though this weary sphere may be not dear,
    I mostly felt above it;
'Cause for any style of domicile
    somewhere are those who love it.
As for me, you know, 'twas long ago
    I retired my walking boots,
And, as it should, *any* place looks good
    when one stops to grow some roots.

TWENTIETH CENTURY CYCLE   1988

For more than half a century when beverages were sold,
the sodas, beers, and milk folks drank most often, we are told,
were put in heavy bottles which by hand and lung were blown,
thus costing far too much for all but bottlers to own.
So when the contents were consumed, in the thoughtful days of yore,
the bottles for deposit, then, were taken to the store;
the store in turn returned them to the beverager, who then
could wash them and refill them ever to be used again.

But in the nineteen sixties, lo, the bottle makers said,
with fast machines and tempered glass the process can be sped,
producing bottles cheaply and by millions every day;
you needn't bother washing, they'll be simply thrown away.
But after twenty years municipalities took note
that nowhere in their boundaries was a place enough remote
to hide the miscreation of the mountains made of trash,
that stood to mar the landscape as a continental rash.

So now there's a necessity to limit landfill mass;
and one way we can do it is recycle all the glass.
It may occur to someone, though, when fuel supplies are short,
that melting of old bottles is an asinine resort.
And furthermore, the labor in the sorting at the bins
with shipping to the glass mills, guarantees that no one wins.
So I expect that someone will remarkably deduce
that washing out old bottles makes more sense for their reuse.

IN PRAISE OF SO-CALLED MUSIC   1989

Although I'm no musician there's a lusty love to sing;
it's a passion and a right to which tenaciously I'll cling;
for many an emotion, as we daily plug along,
is vented in an outburst of invigorating song.

The comedian, Jack Benny, spite of amateurish din,
claimed foremost dedication as a man of violin.
"Who else", asked he, as criticism stoically was weathered,
"would continue to keep playing after being tarred and feathered?"

A lavatory sink we used possessed an eerie drone
as water through the service pipe produced a haunting tone;
so when it filled, and thus began the plumbing song to rise,
would you believe I couldn't resist the urge to harmonize?

We had a hunting dog which, when a marching band would play,
would lend its voice to join them as he loudly bayed away.
Annoyed? Or gaily singing? The latter, we believe,
for it could have bitten someone, and was always free to leave.

There's music when we want it, as for some of us at least,
we try our best to make it, be we person, thing, or beast;
we sing to make us happy, to create a state of mirth,
and find music where it happens, to enjoy for all it's worth.

Published in *THE POETS' TOUCHSTONE*

THOUGHTS ON TACITURNITY 1989

Some years ago I knew a quiet child
who sometimes was inclined to stare and gawk;
it hardly seemed important that he talk,
but grandma got upset and slightly riled.

"Cat got your tongue?" she always had to say;
"Cat got your tongue?" without an end it seemed,
until at length one night he sadly dreamed
a cat, indeed, did chew his tongue away.

An older youth I knew thought talk not cheap,
and rarely ventured anything to say.
The folks assumed opinions lurked, and they
so kindly sawed, "Still water runneth deep".

Though reticence in youth might be behooved,
to some it indicates stupidity;
but better stupid, let them think he be,
then to open up his mouth and have it proved.
(Yeah, yeah, I know Lincoln said this earlier)

A gentleman we know, though speech diminished,
denied to being quiet or less than bright;
he claimed that he was merely too polite
to speak before another person finished.

UP AND DOWN ON GRANITE STREET
1990

While walking one gray day on Granite Street,
and feeling sort of glum and obsolete,
I shuffled down the concrete somberly
when chanced, a lovely lady smiled at me.

My ego felt a moderating boost
as pessimistic thoughts became reduced;
my gloom, however, yet unreconciled,
was dealt a blow—another lady smiled.

Grudgingly my spirits slowly rose;
some mystic charm, the cause I couldn't suppose,
produced results down this street and the next,
delightful damsels seemingly most hexed.

My self-assurance boundlessly had soared
as golden sunshine all about now poured,
enhancing in the windows I would pass
the sight of my reflection in the glass.

Twas then, high at the peak of my aplomb,
which crashed to earth destroyed as by a bomb,
that I, in vivid revelation froze,
To see the greasy smear across my nose.

What had as pleasant flattery been construed,
actually were grins of mirth ensued.
Those smiles, alas, which I so fondly cherished,
faded from my mind—my ego perished.

SUPERNATURALIST'S GOTCHA
June 14, 1993 revised July 4, 2015

We are confident now of the earth's long endurance
though skeptical too of supportive assurance:
gullibility reigns through the whole human race,
of logical sense there is hardly a trace.
Believers in poltergeists, witches, and ghosts
are afraid that their blood will be vampires' toasts.
Superstition lives on to beleaguer our lives
like something an ill-conceived cynic contrives:
the little black kitten all cuddly charm
certainly never meant anyone harm
when it happened in somebody's path to appear
and that person was violently stricken with fear.
Medical amulets sold by the sacks
benefit just by enriching the quacks.
Imagine, indeed, that in this day and age
astrology still is a serious rage.
The list can forever and ever go on:
ignorance thrives and just begs for a con;
paranormal accepted with hardly a fuss,
the world and its people are ready for us.

I'M SORRY FRANKLIN October, 1990

Incident at Tilden School, Keene, N.H. cir 1937

An episode that I recall from school,
An event which, glad to say, was not the rule,
But a case of which I'm not the least bit proud,
Was when us guys just followed with the crowd
And did an act we knew was sort of mean—
There was no chance that we would not be seen.
The fact that we were only ten years old
Is no excuse to leave this tale untold.

For Franklin was a classmate who had had
A bout with polio as a younger lad;
Though handicapped, he stumbled so to mock
On twisted legs a brave attempt to walk,
That some kid, now I can't remember who,
The instigator of our coward crew,
Began a recess recreation that
Was a game of "keepaway" with Franklin's hat.

As nimble feet raced quickly around the yard,
Poor Franklin struggled valiantly and hard,
A few feet forth and then a few feet back,
To chase in vain the boisterous wolf-like pack.
This game, of course, that it not start a trend,
Emphatically came promptly to an end;
And all us guys were duly reprimanded
As severely as our "trespasses" demanded.

But fifty years later now I find
A Franklin retribution on my mind:
For frequently when walking in a rush
Through woods composed of scraggy trees and brush,
A branch will snatch the hat right off my head,
Reminding me of thoughts I've come to dread;
And as this happens almost every day,
"I'm sorry Franklin", must I ever say.

TWEAKING POETS 1991

If poets filled a hippodrome
and forced themselves to concentrate
on which emotion most hits home,
both love and hate should each create
an equal serving on the plate.
For feeling is the gist of song,
yet, love's excess may seem to state:
Ten thousand poets can't be wrong.

So, must we have to search and comb
for poems with a theme of hate?
Except for racists in the tome
of poems in the world to date,
the love is found in dreary sate,
like children, God, and death—too long,
the thesis, love, begins to grate.
Ten thousand poets may be wrong.

Yet poets still, from Rome to Nome,
continue a fantastic rate,
until their bones enrich the loam,
to issue from a flooding gate
their words of love with no abate.
Forever will they go along
by adding to this current spate.
Ten thousand poets must be wrong.

ENVOI

O Prince, we face our hollow fate,
and gladly join the banal throng,
for love will win this non-debate.
Ten thousand poets can't be wrong!

Published by The Goodwin Library
(without ENVOI)

OCTOBER FIRST   May 31, 1991

One month arrives that we are well aware,
for booming noise and rattling shot of lead
announce it, although still we lie in bed.
This is, of course, October, cool and fair,
when hunting season starts with awesome flair
as skirmish lines of shooters stealthily tread,
and before we are even dressed and fed,
the game is dead or driven from its lair.
Yet, I'd have no compunctions to confront,
if this were a necessity to eat.
My father deeply loved the outdoor life
and cherished every chance he had to hunt;
but hunting now seems almost obsolete
when supermarkets everywhere are rife.

JESSICA   1988

Re. television mystery series *Murder She Wrote*
which ran from1984 to 1996

Mrs. Fletcher, we can see all your exploits on teevee,
and I'm proud that I can claim you as my kin;
but since murder is the game which has brought about your fame,
my enthusiastic friendship might wear thin.

Now Jessica, my cousin, you have got the folks all buzzin'
when your annual vacation is at hand;
for we're all a feared of knowing about where you might be going
and in whose household proper you will land.

Of course we love you dear, but the only thing we fear
is that sometime you might take us by surprise.
The problem we have found is whenever you're around,
some poor soul soon meets a quick demise.

You're lovely and your charming with demeanor quite disarming,
you're intelligent, and brave as one can be;
but usually I'm praying that down in Maine you're staying
and, good heavens, that you'll never visit me.

MUSICAL FANTASY (To Eris)

January 31, 1992

He closed up the windows and locked all the doors,
sure no one was present in all rooms and floors,
then approached the piano and took a few bows,
his absentee audience pleased to arouse.
He carefully sat on the polished black stool,
the picture of confidence, gifted and cool,
adjusted his tails in a casual way,
flexed nimble fingers and started to play.

Concertos with frills he heard render the air;
discords with trills were the truth without flair.
His arms flayed with the fury of Valhalla gods,
his head bobbed with vigorous gestures and nods.
As hands met the keyboard, to him most exalting,
collisions, not chords, struck the ears assaulting.
But he sometimes played softly with a beatific smile
some meaningless passage in a contrasting style.

And thus it continued for all of an hour,
with lapses to harmony mixed with the sour,
until he concluded the ultimate bar
and rested his hands from this concert bizarre.
The creaking of heating pipes teasing his ears
became thunderous volumes of bravos and cheers.
No crazier concert has one had to defend;
whatever one's age it is fun to pretend.

RIVER SERPENTS   1992

I am sitting warm and cozy in the van,
while parked upon the Allegheny's shore,
as rain and fog restrict my right to scan
whatever scene I might have viewed before.
The raindrops roughen up the water's glaze,
the fog and mist obscure the farther bank,
then suddenly loom events but to amaze,
and I am taken in by nature's prank.

For, way out near the limit of my sight
there pass a slew of serpents swimming past,
a steady rate parade from left to right,
their undulating bodies never fast.
Some large, some small, and some with heads held high,
and some with tails or bellies in the air,
they swim with mock determination by,
in hopes to reach the Gulf, or who knows where.

Of course, the rivulets of rain that run

on down the windshield in uneven flow,

capriciously adept in causing fun

with logs and limbs that in the current go,

refract the shapes of images I see

to form the writhing monsters of the river.

Such sticks washed in the day before could be

the things that make the superstitious quiver.

Published in *THE POETS' TOUCHSTONE*

BOREDOM February 13, 1993 CAUDA 2015

Sweet ennui, how fortunate I am
to have you when I start the big descent;
for on the climb so much of life is spent
In vigorous ambition to grand-slam.
We build, achieve, acquire, crusade, and cram
the trivia in our heads with full intent
to show significant accomplishment—
as if the whole world really gives a damn.
Time, to busy people, flies so fast
it may have passed before they be aware,
and cause regret from memories too fleet.
But boredom helps us pause to see the past
and analyze the present with a flare
for filling out our lives—if not replete.

       But incomplete,
Regretfulness may quite impede the way—
forgetfulness arrives to save the day.

BELIEF   1995

How often have I read a piece in any publication
wherein some person carries on in utter fascination,
expounding on philosophies and things that really are
to me quite stupid, out of touch and, too, downright bizarre.
Such as, why is some religious thought considered so terrific
just because its roots go back into the Paleolithic?

Belief is why! Belief can make a vapid point of view
seem plausible, acceptable, and very true to you.
So, in avoiding dogma and an orthodox compliance,
I constantly adjust my views to the realities of science.
And my beliefs, so sound and real that others all look pallid,
Are still beliefs, and being such, may really not be valid.

BAH, HUMBLE!   1999

What is one's lifetime to the Cenozoic?
Merely the flash of a firefly in the night!
So few have made accomplishments heroic,
that all self-praise will sound just bland and trite.
Yet, though that flash is vital to the firefly,
and though one's life be bright to him so far,
the flash falls far too dim to light the sky,
and no one in this age ignites a star.
We run a race on foot to find out where
we stand in physical strength against our peers,
or submit our poems to editors if we care
to find our place in intellectual tiers.
Tell you what I'd do if I were God:
The last place guy would always get the nod.

TRAIN WATCHING   1995

I am parked at a station in Greenwich, Cee Tee;
the trains roar by loudly a few feet from me;
they are mostly commuters, the Connecticut Line,
about six to the hour so the rails always shine.
Electrified drive wheels distribute the torque,
propelling the people to life in New York.
Occasionally, though, when a local may stop,
there's a pause in the rush for a passenger drop.
Next, the blast from the Amtrak makes my van sway and shake
as a skiff rocks at dockside from a powerboat's wake.
Some enjoy watching trains, some enjoy viewing art;
those preferring the former are rail fans at heart.

OMENS   1995

As Robert the Bruce observed one night
  a spider spin its thread,
and noted that it failed six times
  connecting overhead;
but when the seventh try was made,
  it fastened to the beam,
and this success to Bruce became
  an omen, it would seem,
Inspiring him to battle, also
  for a seventh try,
and the armies of the English were
  defeated by and by.
Thus, through that little spider he so
  carefully observed,
the Scottish kingdom was, indeed,
  courageously preserved.

So likewise I observed once on
  Nantucket's sunny shore,
a seagull drop a clam that it had
  dropped then twice before;
by flying high above a rock
  a hundred feet or so,
it finally found its aim was true
  and dined back down below.
Then thinking the commercial show,
  the reason we were there,
had not shown much success throughout
  two seasons selling ware;
well, why not give it one more shot,
  the muse of fortune smirks;
and this time we did fairly well;
  by gosh, it really works.

TINKERER'S HEAVEN   1996

There are in this world many stores of renown,
where shoppers and browsers from big shots on down
enjoy finding specialty items they crave
and return from their forays to gushingly rave:

For women of fashion, the swanky boutique
may offer a gown that is chic and unique.
The gourmet, of course, in a thrill-seeking mood
can visit a shop of incredible food.

For computer-expanding electronic buffs
the store for the hackers has more than enough.
And the stodgiest, old-fashioned history freaks
can vent their exuberance seeking antiques.

But my special, huge, overpowering lure:
I am basically simply a tool-fool for sure;
screw drivers, sledge hammers, scroll saws, you see,
all such things seem sort of sacred to me.

And if when I die, for eternity spent
I should hope as an honest reward to be sent
to haunt a Home Depot, the Heaven sublime,
surrounded by hardware forever in time.

SONNET TO POETS, PRO-CON

Their lyrics have for ages entertained,
in stark and colored words their stories sang;
for Kipling, Service, Frost, and all the gang
whose inspirations from wherever obtained
are read with rapture—oft in mind retained;
their tales were told with force of a cannon's bang
and charged with moving clarity that rang,
embellished but with words that most pertained.
However there are some, I feel quite sure,
that bafflement is what they might intend;
I would ascertain their meanings, if I could.
Is poetic merit based on the obscure—
the degree to which one cannot comprehend?
Accolades to those best understood!

CROCODILE KISSES September 30, 1996

(In re. 1929 -1939 Hollywood Hays Office)

The youth in whom testosterone begins
intriguing, subtle whims, desires and fears,
is moved anon, though wet behind the ears,
to certain acts and deeds once known as sins.
And in his quest he learns he seldom wins
by force of lust that spawns resentful tears;
but a gentle kiss may sway the tender dears
to think on lines of peoples' origins.
Then why in many movies recently
does the kissing scene resemble an attack
with lashing tongues and gnashing teeth the style?
It could be done somewhat more decently:
just bring the nineteen thirties love scenes back.
Bah! Who would want to kiss a crocodile?

TO ROBERT FROST 1997

"Something there is that doesn't love a wall"?
Whatever it is, the battle now is done;
those barriers that once stood straight and tall
have tumbled, and the "something" forces won.
The cattle that the fences once contained
no longer roam the pastures and the woods;
those walls the farmers carefully maintained
are sometimes, these days, barely understood.
Indeed, some owners can't recall which line
marks property when several walls exist,
and hope surveyors might somehow divine
the boundary that the present owners missed.
Yes, Mister Frost, you really got it right:
Poor fences get them spoiling for a fight.

CONCEIT   February 28, 1997

We are, it seems, a supercilious race,
a race that must employ whatever means
to glorify and propagate its genes,
as if we be essential to replace.
So, on we go at some most rapid pace
down reproductive roads where life careens
and little to restrain it intervenes.
Lest, egad, we die and leave no trace.
Why not? The full-maned lion takes this ride
when winning over another lion's pride;
then filled with verve his own conceit inspired,
he kills the cubs his predecessor sired.
If nature's excess vanity be the thing,
could be the way one gets to be the king.

Published in *THE POETS' TOUCHSTONE*

SHOOTING INCIDENT

August, 1999

As boys in nineteen thirty nine could do,
we sometimes took our twenty twos in hand
and hiked the woods in hopes perhaps a few
tin cans might be plinked around the land.
Well, opportunity or lucky chance
presented us live game to test our skill.
My friend Bobby spotted on a branch
a large red squirrel he might attempt to drill.
So Bobby down below took careful aim
and fired one shot so unexpectedly well
that I have never after felt the same—
because not one, but two red squirrels fell.
The implications of such cruelty wrought
enhance what every pacifist has taught.

THE GYPSY MOTHS

1988, revised 2010, revised 2014

The infestation back in eighty-two
of caterpillar armies in the trees
defoliating forests by degrees
'till everywhere the sun blazed brashly through,
was, they told us, just a cycle that
would end itself within three years or so;
but how it would they didn't seem to know.
It sounded like mere wishful idle chat.

The hairy larva, soon we came to hate them;
we saw them, heard them, smelled them and took care
when leaning against a tree that none be there.
A browsing pony shuddered when it ate them.
In August when the moths were on the go,
a winter scene anomaly was found,
as males seeking mates would flit around
the barren trees like flakes of sticky snow.

Eventually this plague did go away,
and not because of predators, nor wide
dispersal of a noxious pesticide,
but from disease. It's nature's way, they say.
Perhaps here lies an omen we should face,
as people overpopulate this sphere,
there's something to give pause if not a clear
consideration of our reckless pace.

LIMERICK October, 1989

A man who lived in a castle
was faced with a horrible hassle:
he tried and tried
but he couldn't decide,
should a flag fly on top or a tassel.

EMPTY INN   September 30, 2003

We stepped into the long deserted inn,
the dusty foyer's welcome uninspired,
the registration signing unrequired.
No guests are warmed with drams of ale and gin;
the bustling for their needs but muted din.
Now, chefs and waiters long ago retired,
the kitchen range remains for years unfired;
and naught to feed a roach within the bin.
In retrospect we see the happy times,
the laughter, warmth, and service with a smile,
provided by the able staff and hosts.
Though more like vague and distant pantomimes,
and all of them so very much worthwhile.
Memories are ghosts, mere wispy ghosts.

LOVERS' LANE   2004

It was springtime in Surry, the midst of a thaw,
though the trails in the flood plain could be traveled, he saw;
for the snow was most gone, but the earth still held frost,
and 'twas time to recover the ground he had lost.
Well, he loved to go smooching the girl he adored,
but her father's front parlor was a place to be bored.
So with fervid affection their natural trait,
they eagerly ventured a Saturday date
to the old lovers' lane in the valley below,
with love in their hearts and their eyes all aglow.
But they failed to consider yon flood control dam
might place them that night in a bit of a jam;
for the hills in the watershed, still deep in snow,
were pouring out water in copious flow.

And the amorous sweethearts oblivious yet,

were suddenly aware of their feet getting wet.

One thing was for sure, it was time to depart:

but imagine the horror when the car could not start!

So they waded in ice water up to their thighs

while musing the lesson of being unwise.

But mostly they rued and would never repeat

opportunity lost them by getting cold feet.

(by morning the car was submerged)

Based on item in The Keene Sentinel

ABOUT THE AUTHOR

Roy Kingsbury Piper was born in Keene, New Hampshire in 1928 on a record-setting windy day. In 1950, he graduated from Brown University, then spent nearly two years in the Philippines with the Army Corp of Engineers during the Korean War. He met his future bride, Anne, in New Jersey, they married in 1956, and then had four children after returning to his home town. Roy worked as a Land Surveyor until he retired in the 1990s, then he and Anne traveled the eastern United States showcasing fine antiques. This is when he honed his skills in verse. Roy is a member of the Poetry Society of New Hampshire, and has been writing poems for his friends, family, and seven grandchildren for as long as anyone can remember.

www.ingramcontent.com/pod-product-compliance
Lightning Source LLC
Chambersburg PA
CBHW031631040426
42452CB00007B/782